NoVA Bards 2022

Edited By Nick Hale

NoVA Bards 2022

Copyright © 2022 by Nick Hale

Nick Hale: Editor, Compiler

James P. Wagner (Ishwa): Associate Editor

Layout Design: Nick Hale

Cover Art: Vincent (VinVulpis) Brancato

Published by Local Gems Press

www.localgemspoetrypress.com

www.novabards.com

www.meetup.com/Northern-Virginia-Poets/

For all the poets,
the lovers of poetry,
and poets' lovers.

Foreword

NoVA Bards has come a long way since its inception. It seems like only yesterday I registered for Meetup and put out the call for submissions for the first NoVA Bards. At our first meeting- not quite a workshop- there were four of us: three poets and one guest. I was the last one to get there and the venue was closed for renovations. We have grown steadily since then.

In 2015, we launched the first volume of NoVA Bards at Anita's in Chantilly, in a room we've long since outgrown. Despite the challenges oof the past few years, we've continued to grow as a community as well as individual poets.

As the world gets back to normal and we get back to live events, our community is stronger than ever. I'm looking forward to seeing every-one in person again as we get back to live events. Of course, we will continue to take advantage of the virtual events that got us through the past two years as well.

The amazing poetry in this volume is a testament to the resilience and talent of the Northern Virginia poetry community. I hope you enjoy reading through it as much as I have.

-Nick Hale

Table of Contents

Joanne Alfano

Wordplay

As I read my poem.
I bear down on the words and phrases.

HerStory zooms across a digital table:
a fable about mothers and daughters
alive with periodic bleeding and laughter--
Now, that would have been the mother
of all origin stories!

Instead its twisted roots cry out
for unnamed women whose blood
flowed through centuries of patriarchy,
suppression, and violence

Men have weaponized the fetus for
domination of the woman's body,
while they ignored bloody coat hangers
on the bathroom floors.

Now, our roots are showing
through the struggle, that
a truly equal society is rarer than
...than anything, ever.

as revealed in the poem
that barely made it to paper
before I read it to a group of friends

who read everything from it,
even beyond what I wrote there

MICHELLE BAKER

I Can't Sleep

I can't sleep.
Here alone.

I can't stop dreaming about you.
Here alone in this bed.

I can't understand, why.
I am here alone.

Without you.

Dennis Barnes

To David

For five centuries
you have stared
at an unseen target
except nothing is there.

Your eyes eager
to grow old,
sense that it is a time
for all ages.

A sling shot drapes
over your shoulder
ready for the stone
that you hold.

You wait for Goliath
to remove his helmet
and expose
a soft temple area.

The stone
almost wills itself
to be cast
in a great success.

Our stares merge
and time pauses,
even though
the tour departs.

We remain frozen
as statues
and stare and stare...
until I blink.

MICHELE BARON

scales

how much memory do we hold in our skin?
pack into our nerve endings?
program into our neurons?

how much is conjured
sweeping fingers across shoulders
tracing lips with tongue
remembering feelings never felt at all
but only ghosted
from online
somewhere
faceless
voiceless
intangible
unaccountable
poetry without words
sadness
without surcease

CL Bledsoe

My Sister's Grief

Is a full glass on wobbly legs,
hovering over a laptop she can't
afford to replace.

Is a phone call to make sure
'm not driving after my second
drink.

Is a fast thing, red and darting,
whereas mine is slow and well-fed.

Rides quietly beside her but mumbles
just out of hearing when she's trying
to get home from work.

Is a card in the mail, left on the table
to be opened.

Is a ringing phone that might be work.

Sits with her when she finally has time
to eat but doesn't speak.

Asks her how her day has been and talks
over the answer.

Settles in while she's making dinner. It has
stories to tell, but remembers them all wrong.

Reminds her after the sun brightens
the morning: I am here.

KC Bosch

The Teachings of the Houdini Family

I did a full inspection after purchasing
my house in Oak Shade. Up in the
attic I found a box of books.
Half about spiritual enlightenment.
Titles such as
"The Shambhala dictionary
of Buddhism and Zen", "Healing
Mantras" "A path of mindfulness"
The rest of them a different
sort of learning.
"Emergency war surgery"
"Criminal law handbook"
"Survival poaching"
"Knife throwing for
sport and defense".
Oh and my favorite
"The complete book of meat"
I read bits of both sides,
The Buddhist speak about being
noble and gentle.
The knife book teaches the different
between throwing a bayonet
or a short dagger.

The meat book taught me
just how different our food sources
are today compared to 1963
when it was published.
The official mail that came for
the previous occupant taught me
that maybe the law handbook was
his best investment.
I am sure it was a he.
I asked my neighbors about
him. None really knew anything
about the family except that they
vanished one night.
Nobody saw them leave.
I did keep the books,
and for a long time,
I also locked my doors.

SHEELAGH CABALDA

Morning rise

the morning grind
the aroma of kapeng robusta
as i press my coffee
i take comfort
in my rise and shine elixir
a necessary treat
amidst the pressure of our collective trauma
this covid pandemic
the endless gun violence
the light rain outside my kitchen window
greets me easily at the breakfast table,
reminds me to breathe
and moves my pen along on a wayfaring journey
as i struggle through my moving mist
and remember it is a brave
and radical act of devotion
to set a tender intention and sigh
let me breathe only love
in this moment
and watch how the tears fall and let go

ADINA CASSAL

Rhymes and Reasons

What is the difference
between turning beauty into fear
and turning fear into beauty?

Ask a poet for answers.
Ask a builder for rhymes.

Plastic decoy swans
glidiing on the pond,
lovely, elegant and evocative,
keep Canada geese away.

Closer to the shore
lotuses cover the surface.
Aren't these flowers
symbols of tranquility, strength,
and transcendence?

An unhurried beaver
reaches for the ample leaves
and with his wet and nimble hands
folds leaf after leaf in half
and then in fourths

and eats them.
Ask an atheist for prayers.
Ask the water for reasons.

Luciano Castellani

Gold

This time, my rhymes are aimed at the material shrines
So many minds idolized to excavate beneath the lies.
To unearth a dirt disguise, purpose to alert the wise,
and avert the eyes from the false treasure or prize.
It's broken down for those that think that they're above
This middle man whom you can't belittle when you've sprung on a love
of loot
You prostitute your soul for gold like it's your only goal, it's
The reason too many lawns are riddled with potholes.
Allow me to repeat my thesis abbreviated.
Unearth, Alert, Avert sight from the deceitfulness of
Riches, which is cause for me to emit this.
I wrote this covered with hopes of prevention.
You put your confidence in cold cash and coal
When the pressure of life won't prevent your fold.
This goes out to those that gave up on the game
Because a diamond ain't nothing but a rock with a name.
Such an unimportant thing, but the bling is blinding,
How ironic is the concept of conflict diamonds?
The struggle is inner and outer - hear and applaud
If you're chasing fool's gold you've bought into a facade.
Men and women need to get it together!
The shame that they gain as they sell rocks for their true treasure -

If you never get anything else I emit, know this:

They stripped them of a continent and got rich.

And the golden legacy of this is proudly worn on necks and wrists

Notice the placement; modern day slavery exists.

And there is no ignorance to this form of self-hatred,

Especially when the parasitic is perpetuated

From people seeking solace of reaping the woes of what was sold to'em

Outsides ballin' but insides broken.

See through the bluff with me as they toast their opulence, yet

Live for nothing.

Adam Church

Because Damage is Best Kept in Good Company

And it all still makes no sense.
We try to be better,
but it all just falls down.
In the end, these towers
of trying to be people crumble.

Imagine the world with
only those we trust.
It may be empty,
but it is comfortable in its solidarity.

Someday they will fix us,
and we will have our scars.
But the blood shed will be over.
I got your back and you got mine.
That is all that matters.

Because damage...
...is best kept in good company.

MIKE CROGHAN

alone

i would write for you
a poem of protection
from the loneliness that gnaws
like bored and empty rats
at the bones of your contentment

i would weave for you
a cloak of connection -
a poem whose words fly out
like a garment's sweeping corners
embracing strangers walking by

i would cook for you
a stew of satisfaction
thick and savory with language
that would fill the hollow spaces
within your body of solitude

but this poem
is just an idol to isolation
only an unwelcome reminder
of the emptiness that yawns inside
our life together, alone

ANANT DHAVALE

Abode

Rains have touched
Your pure skin

Winds have flown through your
Hair

Earth has lingered in your
Being

Your bosom, the
Resting abode of this
World

Rudy Diaz

Desolate white crystal trees left in the void of an early morning
On Cemetery's Road
Dancing with the dead

The man flees his broken palace leaving residue of himself
Everything left behind on his search to desire nothing once again
A child's head floating through the breeze

John Donley

Driving on Empty

Yesterday's wake disappears
Into the eyes open now
Yearning to fill each next day
With enough activity
To please the wont of being
Driving is mostly alright
Staying between the white lines
Eyeing the live garmin screen
The blue arrowhead floating
On the bright pink road ahead
Assessing time remaining
To today's destination
Three rear mirrors reflecting
Triangulating motion
Set to reevaluate
Matter's place in time and space
Allowing mind's eye to drift
Upon wisps of emotion
Conjured by the radio's
Stray alarm clock from the past
Resonant rhythms ringing
Waking visceral echoes
Sipping fresh bittersweet tears

Accepting pangs of sorrow
Dipping into wells of joy
Affirming a thirst for love
Unsatisfying in depth
Too fragmented to relive
Mislaid passion gone like smoke
Still alive on cruise control
Among columns of drivers
Each in silent thought enclosed
Rolling into each moment
Maintaining linear pace
Convinced serendipity
Lies on the road just ahead

A.M. Donovan

Pride

Wait for me
I long to cry
Don't leave me
I'll come
But stubborn pride
Holds still my tongue
And I'm alone
Again

Ask again
I will say yes
Just ask again
I can't

I will not beg
I will not cry
"Please don't leave"
I cannot say

I won't say go
I can't say stay
Oh, can't you see
My breaking heart
Needing you

Stubborn pride
Won't let me say it

John Dutton

Home

As I lie exhausted on the couch,
I dwell in slovenly comfort
During the final hours
Of another satisfyingly
frustrating day.
I know not every task was completed,
Yet something was checked off
The never-ending
"To-Do" list of life.
I find comfort around me
And think,
"Home is where the heart is."
Clothes strewn on the floor.
Books piled in every nook.
Dog curled on my lap.
TV murmurs in the background.
Kids stomping the stairs.
Dishes stacked precariously.
Mismatched socks seeking lonely shoes.
Toys in every corner.
Wife reading in her favorite chair.
My coffee cup in hand.
I exhale and let the day fall from my shoulders.
I have found comfort in the clutter.

Danielle Erwin

Mama (6/22/19)

See the clouds in the sky
With the sun peeking through
That's me, mama
Talkin' to you
Peering through the darkness
That little light
Is me, mama
Watchin' tonight

I know you miss me, mama
I know you long to hold me close
I see you desperately,
Wishing you could count my toes
I'm watchin' for ya, mama
When you get to the end of your road
It's me, mama, waitin' for you

I left a little early
Sorry I left you alone
God called, mama
So I had to go
He gave me to you and
I made you smile

Don't worry, mama
It's only a while

I know you miss me, mama
I know you long to hold me close
I see you desperately,
Wishing you could kiss my toes
I'm watching for ya, mama
When you get to the end of your road
I'm here mama, waitin' for you

Even though we're so far apart, mama
I'm alive there...in your broken heart

Though you miss me, mama and
Though you long to hold me close
I'm here prayin' for ya, mama
Through your highs and lows
I'll be waitin' for ya, mama
When you reach the end of your road
No rush mama, I'm waitin' for you

Yeah, It's me mama, waitin' for you

ALEXIS FERNANDEZ

I've been having restless nights wondering if i done wrong,
But I have to keep up the fight cause i was raised strong,
Many people don't understand how this man formed,

with the struggles that depressed any feeling of success, I've over-
came and became a man with ambitious to possess anything that life
has blessed.

And i keep transforming, i keep on growing
Cause it's the hunger of a better life for those i love that keeps me
going,

And when i see the light ill run to it, i'll follow it, and when that pride
hits i'll swallow it, i'll bottle it..

Because there is no room for pride,
When your actions bring consequences so the ones you love could
thrive,
And i see there's bluer skies,
When i fight with effort for those that in me rely.

It's easy to fall into darkness and sadness,
Losing ourselves into insanity or madness,

But all i have to do it's believe in me, and have faith that all that i envision will come to be,

Cause faith is all that we possess, when things don't come around how we predicted they might come to manifest,

but that's life taking unexpected turns, some where we might get burned, some where there is no return, leaving us with more concerns, testing how much we've grown,

But we take those chances and we run with them and follow them, And when those bad turns come, we will swallow them and learn from them,

Cause those are lessons that life will bring,
Lessons that are harsh and they will sting,
But without does lessons that life will spring,
Without you feeling that bitter sting,
Without you learning from what they bring,
Your life will not move forward to greater things.

And as we get old, with each step life will unfold,
showing us paths that are untold, guiding us through to find our souls,

Live, learn and love, keep fighting for what's above, keep struggling for those you love,

Your reward will come with lessons learned,

When you feel the struggles and how they've turned

To the life lessons that you've learned unfold,

Reaping the fruits of what you've solved,

And showing that your sacrifice was worth it all.

And because of the love that my family infects,

I became the man that my family respects.

DEBORAH E. FEUTI

Appalachian Spring

My Darling,
It's that time of year again:
When the whippoorwill sings in the morning
Bluebirds fly through the house without warning.
The field grass grows as thick as snow
And the inspiration finally begins to flow.
The silence of winter that I abhorred
Is now disguised by the pond frogs roar.
Lady Sunshine is at the end of the lane
Her spirit broken from life's hard strain
Clearly weeping, as the willow sways
A gentle breeze owns the day.
This year, this time, this spring
And just as before, time and time again
So lost and yet so very found
In the simple harmony...
Of natures sweetest sounds.

ROBERT FLEMING

7 wonder witch spells

telekinesis
use it in a sentence
move a child into a pot
use it in a spell
no this is a spelling bee
spell transmutation instead?
no
concilium change the spell word in your mind
divination – u judges bought lottery tickets
gossip
set u on fire
pyrokinesis go ahead fire extinguisher on wall
vitalum vitalis – spell only one word
descensum – bring back your husband from hell
o.k. substitute transmutation

Rich Follett

tubular vision

he was
a crazy man --
designed to feint and flail,
his outward self
(can a nylon cylinder have a self?)
a mirror image of
my inner bedlam

on the cell
with a friend
in the ell of a strip mall parking lot
picking up chinese take-out
with crazy man gyrating wildly
in the periphery,
i could not bring myself to
step out of the car

a vomitous, malignant rage was
darkening, swelling into
virulent parallax anguish
when, in the throes of
what could only have been
unprecedented celestial alignment,

crazy man tucked his head
under the eaves
and was briefly,
inexplicably
still ...

if he,
conceived for chaos,
could find even
the merest moment of
sanctified quietude,
how dare i persist
in psychic
entropy?

ERIC FORSBERGH

Zipper

Because you asked what route this was
as he stood waiting for a bus,
his smile an easy crease
piquing your interest, this led you
to find him once again. Then,
you impressed your smile
on his memory like a key in wax
and three months later he waits quietly
in the dark as you slowly unzip
yourself and two years later
you are pregnant.
                You are reminded of
that winter in Genetics class, how
chromosomes unzip and now
yours and his clasp into someone
by now the size of a walnut,
this half-and-half agreement, so far
your blood-and-flesh imaginary friend.

34

GREG FRIEDMANN

New Languages

They say you should learn new languages
as you age, to keep your mind sharp—so
I'm taking up meadowlark, as I wish to know
her word for the bright yellow of her breast.
I am learning barred owl, to assure him that
no one cooks for me and ask him how
he finds unseen gaps in thick, dark woods.
I am working to translate the river's burbling
to know how the past becomes the future.
I am studying the dialects of cloud and sky
to understand their perfect marriage.

KIMBERLY GILLIAM

The Watchers

Pine needles on the sidewalk,
Sometimes small branches from the storm,
More debris as I walk to the corner to turn.

As I approach, I sense them
The light changes and darkens.
The temperature drops,
I look up, I see them.

The Watchers,
Always there rooted
In the same dirt I walk on.
They stand, they see.

They see the rabbits in the morning,
The woman passing with her dog,
The lovers, kissing at the bend;
And the man, who runs the stop sign.

For a hundred years, silent
Gathering and keeping secrets.
The only sound they make is
The wind running though the branches,

Like a child playing in a maze.
Arms stretched over me,
I feel their protection.
I stop and look up,
I say thank you...
Then, continue, on my walk.

LEIGH GIZA

Journaling the Journey

April 10, 2020
Washing hands hourly
Getting tested frequently
Fretting constantly

April 10, 2021
Buying s**t online
Eating just to pass the time
Going stir crazy

April 10, 2022
Masking when shopping
Getting a second booster
Will this ever end?

KATHERINE GOTTHARDT

APPetite

Open the app to curiosity.
Actively seek the purposeful glitch
in otherwise perfect lines.
Catch a whiff of anomaly
creativity set free
in a repetitive universe.
Enjoy the reprieve
from sense and logic as you know it.
Put it in your mouth. Chew on it.
That mysterious candy, poetry.

CATHY HAILEY

Summer Rain

Dawn sneaks in without fanfare,
the sun's yellow rays
hiding behind grays.
Drops trickle from treetops
sounding like new rainfall
as squirrels play tag
in a gray-barked leafless tree.
With a sudden sprint,
they disappear, perplexing
witnesses until the intruder
slinks out from behind
Hostas and potted plants—
a furry-tailed fox
hungry for his own gray meal.

NICK HALE

2020 is a Gift

It may not seem like
hidden fringes
the prize we have to work for
bottom of the cereal box
in a world where trophies
are free
the quest for the blessing
is its own kind

we are not drowning
thirsty- desiccated
we sneeze in the
inferno
we swallow the fetid
boon of an ungrateful spring
against our better reason
to save our better angels

this is how growth happens
the line goes
we grow together
apart
from the safety

of our own airspace
we learned the lessons
we missed last time
all the times before
we fell for
life's sleight of hand

This is a gift.

DEBORAH HARTMAN

Let George Be George

They do not want any more bedtime stories.
They are ready to read and to write their own stories.
And to be left alone, except when they need you.

I miss the adventures with Curious George and
Saying good night to the moon.
I miss the schoolgirls all in a line,
And the smallest one
Little Madeline.

I miss the songs and stories,
Fairy tales and rhymes.
Good night songs, hugs and kisses
So long lost in time.

Still it's hard for me to turn off the light,
Knowing that sometimes, my youngest
May have a bad dream and call out for me.
Until, that too, becomes something else
She will keep inside.

Maybe I need to be like
The Man in the Yellow Hat.

Concerned, but not worrying too much.

Letting Curious George

Get into all sorts of mischief,

Yet hoping

For many happy endings.

DANNI HILL

Man In The Moon

Hello Moon, my old friend,
I come to stare at you again.
I ponder and wonder, just like Edgar Allan Poe:
'Aren't thou lonely in the sky, with only stars to keep you by?'
'Aren't thou left as the alone, white candle of the night?'
Your silence amuses me and puzzles me so!
Why don't you answer me, you sullen mime?

No need to convey with your glistening brightness
I need your comforting words,
to sooth this inner distress!
I shall send out an SOS to your moon madness
to let thou know I'm coming for thee,
with a raven as our witness for this midsummer's night.
I'm building myself a ladder
where my hands shall touch thee,
so that I'll forevermore be tainted by your darkness!

Tis, I'm aware, my hands shall forever be unclean,
by the blood I spill to get to thee
Everything comes with a price like a Grimm's fairy tale,
but a sin of loneliness changes a person overnight!

Tim Hoffman

Something Like a Train

by Tim Hoffman
We had a freight line
running through nearby,
on the far side of a little ball field
in front of our house,
and at night
the rhythm of the coal cars
and long, moaning whistles
constantly seeped into my dreams.
Often, I would awake
for a moment to listen,
like a secret between just us,
and knowing we didn't have long
I would ask the train
where all this rock was heading to
and where it would ultimately burn.
I wondered when it would be my time
and what sights I might see
and what adventures I might have
before my turn.
And the train, while
keeping to its schedule—
keeping to kept to

keeping to kept to
keeping to kept to
keeping to kept to—
at times offered me
a hint of an answer,
just a glimpse.
But mostly the train stayed aloof
and mysterious,
and I'd drift back off to sleep
to the sound of hissing tracks
as its last cars passed away.

CHRISTPHER J. HOH

Leave the Leaves

Leave it be or let it be?
Grammar's conundrum goes well beyond me!
Leaves from trees that fall in fall,
Them I relate to, leaf-mold and all.

Experts remind us to let the leaves lie;
Leave them alone breaking down by and by.
Nature's own mulch saves on funds and on toil;
Leaves decomposing aids plants and their soil.

Now those leaf-blowers with noise and foul fumes,
Leave them off; let peace resume.
May these small scribblings help us to see —
Autumn leaves, just let them be.

EMILIO IASIELLO

Breakfast at Metro 29

I spend a lot of time here now that you're away.
The waitress recognizes my face,
her eyes bright with acknowledgement.
She leads me to our table where
I drink coffee after coffee
substituting nourishment with caffeine.
My appetite has vanished since you left,
leaving me crumpled and stained,
an unpaid check.

When you return we'll eat like we used to:
scrambled eggs and flapjacks smothered
in maple syrup, the butter sweetening
on our tongues. You'll order
freshly squeezed OJ and greasy home fries
and we'll feast while we reassemble
our lives like we used to -

one forkful at a time.

Brian Donell James

Understanding

I clip gray hairs from my goatee to preserve myself
When my vision becomes blurry I know to check my blood pressure
I am notorious for having full blown conversations by myself
And the crashes of things thrown can be heard periodically

Hours on the clock mean nothing to me
I am up late due to never ending deadlines, in my mind
And I snore loudly in mornings, noon, and at night
Whenever the mood comes
My family simply shuts the bedroom door
And braces for impact

Perhaps soon they will commit me
To a lovely physicality with manicured lawns

Perhaps they'll spring for a jacket that straps me in tight
From the back, You know,
So that I can stay warm

Or perhaps they will leave a poet at bey

Because I'm happy in my craziness

Crafting words of life, against this living death

Where I cannot escape the beauty of art

This poetic pain and joy

We have an understanding.............

Jodie James

Lemonade

Theresa spins the dial on my radio.
Holly rolls the windows down.
I do the turn signals and drive the car around.

We sing to old pop punk songs
And take turns yelling along.
I never drive
-But I volunteered tonight-
And it feels nice, for the first time in a long while.

When we get home
We spend a half hour in the parking lot.
I dance in the car and forget to feel awkward about it.
This existence comes easy.
Like sharing lemonade,
Just enough sugar to drown the bitterness of its rarity.

We are alive in summertime.
I am alive at 22,
With friends I have know for less than a year.
I have not had lemonade since middle school,
But tonight all there is is water, and sugar, and fresh fruit.

I mix a little love into my glass and share it with you.

When the lemons fall from the tree,

I'll still have you and you'll still have me,

And Thursday will still taste as sweet.

John Johnson

Imposter Syndrome

Stealing state secrets, a double agent.

Clasping the clipboard, the backup quarterback.

Is he a real doctor? the Chiropractor.

Remarkable resemblance to Richard Simmons, a doppelganger

Masking your lousy argument, emphatic gestures.

Off the medal stand, the fourth-place finisher.

Regretting his words were purchased, the Ghost writer.

Possessing your password, a hacker.

Craving meat, an Impossible burger.

An abecedarian poem starting with J, Imposter Syndrome.

In an undisclosed location, Kamala Harris.

Anxious afterthought, the last friend invited.

Terrified of beard tuggers, a mall Santa Claus.

Police Academy dropout, the night-shift security guard.

Waiting for him, the "other" woman.

Nigerian businessman needing your bank account number, a phishing email.

Hocking age defying skin creams, a quack.

Not Ronald Reagan, Rich Little.

Listening to Mozart, Salieri.

Celebrating with horses, Trojans

Envy of ovations, the understudy.

Loose lips, a ventriloquist.

Dry heat again, a weatherman in Phoenix.

Originals signed, Xerox copies

Bounced by a fake ID, underage youth.

A funny tasting cucumber, it's zucchini.

RICHARD "ERIC" JOHNSON

Make a Move

crossing double yellow lines
weaving around orange cones
under white lettered green signs
denying distances and arrows

concrete dirt
asphalt brick
off road grass
shore line sands

forking roads everywhere
here there nowhere
above night day sky
stars behind any fog

I dare you
double dare you
just touch me
sea what happens

KATHY WALDEN KAPLAN

The Tall Girl

The tall girl
kneads clay—
　a base
　a cradle
to hold the uplift
where hands hover,
bless the mud.

Leah Kim

Interrupt the Sonnet

there are two cardinals
in the pear tree

and from far away,
they disrupt the quiet greenery.

roses, they're like roses.

i wonder where the thorn would be
on a cardinal rose.

i wonder if i could put a cardinal
in a birdcage

and it'd be like

making a bouquet.

(i watch the cardinals
fly away.)

KATHLEEN KINSOLVING

What Makes a Martyr

Flesh doesn't matter
Like fear, it falls away
Replaced by obedience
To noble oblation.

In the offering
Of a surrendering soul
Horrors dissipate
As the body burns
Or starves
Or drowns.

In martyrdom
Pain is trivial
It only serves as a price
For the grace of sacrifice.

Lucy Koons

Jet Lag

I kind of like the texture of this in-between,
like static on an old TV after midnight,
when networks went from slick air-time to scratchy snow,
from national anthem to quiet latitude.

My circadian rhythm drums a morning beat
but, alas, the sun has yet to shadow the dial,
this eastward shift a languid wait for longitude.

I kind of like this in-between, but not forever.

TORI KOVARIK

Broken Pinecone

From its spinal core, it flowered, petals opening
and graying. Stepped on, damaged,
the petals loosed like baby teeth,
ripe for the pulling and fidgeting.
Plucked from their places, they have left
a gap-toothed spine that grimaces,
showing off the hue of gum's sticky blood-sap,
smelling of the destructive act.

Tisha Kramer

Middle Age

Every time I say goodbye
To a loved one now,
It's not with that youthful reassurance
That I'll see you later.
It's with this unwanted knowing
And a nagging sadness,
that perhaps it may be the last.
And how very grateful I am
For this goodbye.

KAREN KROTZER

Lonely Lawn Chairs

Brown metal lawn chairs
Left outside year-round
Unprotected from the elements.
They huddled together for warmth,
Poised ready for gossip and chatter
That would accompany warmer weather.
For now they attempt
To entice human company
With inviting white cushions
Freshly laid from the last snowfall.

Previously published in *Rhyme Time,* Volume 7, Number 1 Jan/Feb 1988

M.Y. Lavoie

The Wild Hunt

I look into your dark eyes, love
And see the riders fly
Through mist and wind and trampled souls
I can hear their shrieking cries.

I marvel in the Wild Hunt
In its race past land and time
I see its fearsome, feral fight
To reclaim the world that was mine.

Your iris is the ground they bound across,
Your pupil the full moon that looms,
I see over the summer horizon
The right that no one assumes.

The skeletal faces aghast,
wrath echoes through their eyes.
I step into the wind of terror
And listen to their striking vies.

For the Wild Hunt has hailed and arrived,
To proclaim some magnificent catastrophe,
The world screams in terror,
But I sense no agony.

The Wild Hunt troubles the lands,
And leaves the cities bleak,
Whatever, my dear, you desire,
There is no more for you to seek.

I have seen the Wild Hunt,
I have heard its haunted howls
In the depths of obsidian night
I have seen what it befouls.

The Wild Hunt has always ran
Through your eyes, dark as smoke,
I understand the fear they bring,
And I know the pain they cloak.

I know I am immune, my dear,
As long as the moment stands,
For though the Hunt is in your eyes,
I have hold of your hands.

MARCIA LEFTWICH

The War

There is a war I battle constantly.
There is a war I do not understand.
There is a war I battle constantly, to understand--
That tissue, flesh, blood and bones from which I came,
can swing a sword to
strike me,
cut me,
wound me.

There is a war I battle constantly.
Words as sharp as a machete slicing sugar cane.
The blow is so devastating, there is nothing left to salvage.

There is a war I battle constantly.
On the battlefield I meet my opponents
rejection
criticism
judgment
oppression
control...

There is a war I battle constantly.
There is a war I do not comprehend– how can my origin and host slay continuously
with the gem filled handle of her prolific sword?

There is a war I battle constantly --to riot for the little girl who was abandoned, and not defended --but taught to be seen and not heard to be dressed up like a china doll for all to admire.

There is a war I battle constantly to love unconditionally
when the battle I contend with is to be loved.

There is a war I battle constantly - privately and publicly.

There is a war I battle constantly, nevertheless, I will fight till the end.

K.A. LEWIS

Liquid Light

Water takes shape
in concrete and
inside my skin.

Arms outstretched
wings, I float
watching, as light
draws patterns
on the turquoise painted
pool bottom.

Sunlit shadows
of widening rings
bloom
like cumulous clouds
seen through the window
of an airplane.

Wind stirs the water.
Patterns diffuse
into glimmering fog.

My spirit floats,
borderless.

A plane passes far overhead.

Pardee Lowe Jr

Contrails

Our lives are like jet contrails
Events first arraying themselves
Tightly in time and space –
White dots against a deep blue sky –
Splaying ever more widely
Till they evanesce
Into the fulness of Eternity

Appeared in Pardee Lowe, Jr. *Openings: Messages in Poetry from Quaker Worship*. Quaker Heron Press. 2021

Louis Mateus

E

I was stopped at the turning lane
to a small highway in my way to work
when a cargo-like plane flew overhead.
On its belly, along its length, a word was painted.
I had time to make out only the first letter
because the driver behind me honked.
The plane hovered over the highway
like an overloaded stork with its landing gear
readying for landing, and I wondered
what the word was on its belly.

Empire, E-Commerce.

What word of advertisement was there
to take my attention off the road like all
the words and images competing for my attention
on the internet, but more dangerously.
I was actually moving on that highway.
But then again, when pressing on
the laptop's pad as the prompt on the screen,
like a friendly hand, is poised on top of an icon,
there is an Audubon between my finger
and the effects of pressing that Icon.

71

Buy Buy Buy Buy

Emporium was another word in mind.
but by this time the theme had been established
and I had to get to work. There are things
I want that are as important, if not more,
as the meaning I draw from my job.
Whatever that word, I bought into something.

SINDHU MATHEW

A twisted flower

Following the vines on a sheet
my thoughts
twist a flower
to a crossbow-theory

Allowing conversations
with myself, with ancestors
shored, hushed,
Thoughts borne from a higher plain

As time tweaks thoughts
into knowledge
As facts churn my defenses
Into a speck

I listen -
for stars to speak again
of cavernous promises,
whispering fallacies about tomorrow

While today echos from behind
Of countless truths denied

MEGAN McDONALD

Next Game

In a time of floating bamboo
or rather man-made wind chimes
on a back cement patio
I put away the poker face work mask
that I wore for 40 plus years.
I don't need to bluff my way
through any more meetings
or pretend to take bets
on a losing proposition.
In the button position
I fully buy into new deals
of anything goes.
I hold the kitchen hand of downtime.
No more taking one more cold call.
The last years of gut shot nonstop all in work turned the dream of
someday
to implied odds of not soon enough
too much open-ended work
was heading to a showdown
too many dead man hands dealt.
So for now I am sitting out
and taking a slow play mode
no more straddling life worries.

74

Time will tell what happens
in the next game.

ALAN MEYROWITZ

Each Time I Visit

he complains I held
the reins too tight

kept him back as other boys
would run to Brian's Lake,
fishing there as easy
as the jumping in

So much else has gone—
odd that he remembers such,
a twisted shard of memory

I've learned by now
to go along, not dwell upon
what would move me to regret

were I his father, not his son

Previously Published in *Tempered Runes* (Winter 2020)

Liz Milner

Twisted Trees

Twisted trees, tangled roots,
Just the pits, and never the fruits.
Twisted trees dancin' in the breeze.

They say you reap just what you sow;
I planted a garden but nothing would grow.
Twisted trees dancin' in the breeze.

I planted my garden but nothing would grow,
I planted that garden such a long time ago.
Twisted trees dancin' in the breeze.

Twisted trees, lousy weeds,
Home for the crows and wasted seeds.
Twisted trees dancin' in the breeze.

Made my own bed, narrow and hard,
Deal me the joker, that's my callin' card.
Twisted trees dancin' in the breeze.

Twisted trees, twisted trees
Sighing "How long," in the breeze.
Twisted trees dancin' in the breeze.

Twisted trees, tangled roots,
Just the pits, and never the fruits.
Twisted trees dancin' in the breeze.

ADRIENNE NGUYEN

A 50 Piece Puzzle

So many pieces
So many different parts of me
All tossed together
In this human shaped box
The picture on the front
Complete and smiling
All who bother to look
See the image of the person they think these pieces should be

But these pieces don't seem to fit
They are different sizes and shapes
They are multi-chrome and vibrant
They are utterly void of color or pattern
A few join together easily
Those with curved edges
Worn smooth with the gentle flow of life
Family, friends, simple pleasures
While the rest obstinately resist
They stand out
Rough and jagged
Torn and ripped apart by the cruelties of existence
or the careless regard of others

I stare numbly at the jumble of pieces
Longing for someone with the patience
To gently lift each piece from this box
Without pity or judgement for the gaps and holes
Filling the spaces in with their own essence
Shot through with golden streaks of pure love
To help me see that this haphazard mosaic
Is uniquely and beautifully complete.

GOVINDA GIRI PRERANA

Queue

They are waiting
In the queue

Queue is long
Queue looks endless

Waiting continues
Day and night
Here and there

With hope
Rising in their eyes
They are waiting

They want life
They just want to breathe

It starts raining
It starts thundering
It starts flooding
It starts land sliding

They are waiting
Holding the candle of hope
In the eyes
Which is already tired

How long they have to wait.
Will they survive?
In the queue
Will the hope
Save their life!

Queue is getting longer
Every day
Every minute
Every moment!

SUSAN REXROAD

a frothy occupation

the bubbles have faded to foam
lazily I swirl shapes into the froth
cascading hearts and curving paisleys
the barista of the bathtub

Heather Roelke

Blackhole

A star shining brightly enough to be seen
By all who travel through the galaxy,
Until the light disappears from the scene
Under the pressure of extreme gravity.
Complete ejection of superfluous matter,
Then the mass pulverizes into singularity.
Time speeds up, moving faster and faster,
And outrageous is the escape velocity
Of the material traveling dead ahead
Into the blackhole that is under her bed.

JIM SANDERS

The Black Camaro

A black Camaro
Rumbles down our street
Boom-box booming
Engine growling
It stops in front
Of the house next door
Snarling softly
Roiling the air
Red tail lights shine brightly
Even in daylight
And when its cargo
Approaches the beast,
The long black beast,
A door opens
A girl climbs in
And off it goes
The black Camaro
Growling away
In a streak of motion
Trailed by the sound of its
Boom- box booming.

APARNA SANJAY

Riot

Riot.
Noun: a violent disturbance of the peace by a crowd.

That year, the monsoon destroyed the sun.
We heard the rumors drip loudly on the roof.
They burst out of swollen streets, eroding
our lives into miniscule points of dread.
And mother slept with a kitchen knife under her pillow.

When they came roaring down our street,
she scudded through the back door, thundering
with our heavy bodies out of the tempest.
They tried to break down the gate; it held.
And mother held us under the folds of her saree.

Other monsoons came, and death squalled anew,
to her fermented rancid rhythms; other mothers
rode through the whirlwind, sprinkling sanctuary like liquid sunshine.
Now memory is but a distant drizzle, damp with gratitude.
Does mother still remember the stormy riot in her heart?

JUDITH SHAPIRO

How Could Anyone Know

I saved all of your letters
and old postcards from faraway places
found rummaging around in junk stores

faded blue ink
exotic old stamps
looping, schoolteacher handwriting —

Dearest Edward,
The weather is lovely.
Last night we had crabs for dinner!
Beatrice is learning to swim.
Wish you were here.
Love, Dorothy

Greetings from Mt. Rushmore!
Herbert

and the one with a picture of a man in suit and tie
ape with hands poking through the bars
captioned—giving a gorilla a manicure

I knew they were from you

we were so clever
filled with the exuberance and immortality of youth

we didn't know then
how could anyone know

that one day
there would be no more letters
no more postcards

and life would go on

a Buddhist teacher said keep the heart open
love in death as you did in life

I try
I really try

Ron Shapiro

Retired Ties

Solids and stripes etched in fabric
Once worn daily to the office now
Piled together resembling snakes
Curled one atop the other,
As if an artist's palette tipped
Over bleeding colors revealing
The pain once choking
The neck. Ties no longer worn,
The dress shirt exchanged now
For a t-shirt, the informal dress
Of relaxation, of freedom, of coolness.
Once at a party two couples played
A round of musical chairs, not looking
At each other, not even fighting for a seat.
One woman with legs crossed, arms folded
With her face frozen like the marble
In a museum sculpture, while the other woman,
left hand over her right wrist simply stared across
The room at paint drying to a Frank
Sinatra song. The men dressed in
Business suits, their wallets pulsating
In jacket pockets, dreaming of stocks
And bonds, without any awareness of

The women sitting right beside them.
One day the men will discard their
Ties, tossing them into a pile, only
To be still choked by the coldness
That cashiered their hearts.

Leslie Sinclair

Ode to Discipline

We think you're uppity; now toe the line
and do the tasks your boss expects of you.
You'll manage home and office – both – just fine.
We make up rules, while you will simply "do."

We hired you for your expertise and made
a name for you; don't share what doesn't suit –
you have to understand you are not paid
for doing good, but kissing butt; it's cute.

So, you don't care to smooch my fat behind?
You'll have to pay to keep that attitude –
I can ensure you're totally maligned,
while others show the proper fortitude.

"Excuse me, but will somebody explain
what's in this game for me? Are you insane?"

DAVID STEWART

Dona Nobis Pacem

As a beloved
i descend
to press my dry lips
against your façade

two souls finalized as one
divinity embracing divinity
my adversary now departed
my heart bids you tenderness too late

K.S. Taylor-Barnes

Beautiful Endings

Time moves forward
Like a never-ending
Highway of unknowns
Always shifting
Filled with obstacles
Creating a desire for more
As possibilities withdraw
From the grasp
Of an aging hand
Covered in ashes
From the consuming blaze
Ignited in our youth.

As winter sets in
Vibrant colors dance across the horizon
Reflecting the desire
Unaltered by time
...To be noticed
...To be useful
...To have purpose
Before softly falling
To a final resting place
Where nothing turns to ashes,

Where colors never fade,
And, life never ends.

KATE TODD

Strolls after the Sunshower

Wildflowers romantically twirled and dipped
from ballroom dancing
With the storm's winds
Are now still and dew-laden
And golden at sunset

The first chord of birdsong
Awakens nature's symphony
And tiny three-pronged feet
Form footprints on the sidewalk
Awaiting erasure by sneakers and strollers

SALLY TONER

Winter Sonnet

The poem's final lines, I think they read:
"And God came down to shed a frozen tear
that spring, in warmth, will come and kiss away."
How profound, if in my search I lifted
this from memories stuffed like trash in metal
cabinets in the corners of my study.
"It's winter in here yet," after all.
or so I've learned from tattered textbook pages
words I've read and taught and trod upon.
All I wanted was to find the sonnet,
my first, typeset teenage brilliance, but—
It's gone, like the kid whose work I found
instead. His image, playing Othello on
the steps. Depression was his Desdemona.

LESLEY TYSON

Weightless

it is things i carry
that burden me hamper progress
they fall from numb hands
unnoticed

yet my grip doesn't seem to falter
holding you even when i cannot feel
as though you are my own weight

only in labyrinthine dreams
am i aware of the weight
of your care for me
only in those dark convoluted corners
i begin to doubt whether i can
save either of us

only in those shadowless constructions
do i understand how critical it is
that you reach the safety of daylight
except you won't grasp the chance
of escape i engineer from fantasy
but you must leave the maze without me
know that i will find you when i awake

because even empty-handed
i start everyday
carrying you in my heart

Rebecca Vsigirl

That Terrible Springtime

In That Terrible Springtime
When you were supposed to keep your circles tight
And you breath in your chest you stole mine
With one little line "I like your hair" did I hear that right?

A queer greeting to be sure,
From a girl in the garden, the sun, the soil
Her hair's short, mine's blue- did she, can I infer?
But your aunt is here, and this is our now, would she recoil?

Oh, if I could climb over the garden chain link
Safely into your space buzzing blooming
Off public sidewalk where you're supposed to walk not overthink
Oh, You're holding the shovel but we're both digging

My dog and maskless state insists we leave you to your hole in the ground
So far several feet wide and thigh-length down.

James P. Wagner (Ishwa)

Disposable

A sad irony that we are dedicated
To being a culture of the disposable

Single serving coffee creamers
Single use water bottles
Paper wrappings
Sugar packets
Teabags

Clothing that lives and dies with the current trends
Computers and cars that last only a few years
Software obsolete, every 483 seconds
Time to update yet again
But we've even managed
To master the art
Of disposable people

Swipe right for more profile pics
Sixty-two resumes to fill this job at starting salary
And the perfect packaged
Wrapped in a box
Fair-weather friend

Good for fun times until the first disagreement
Then put back in the box
Tossed into the trash
To buy another
Nearly 8 billion more to choose from
No more patience
For the art of that long-stepped cup of tea and the spiritual experience
that comes with it
The custom tailored suit that fits you like an extension of your body
Or the deep type of human relationship
Where you know eachother inside and out
Your strengths and vulnerabilities
Built on a history
, that makes life worth living

No wonder the average 30 year old
Has fewer people in their lives they can depend on
Than fingers on their right hand

Our existences splashed Into many bodies of water,
All puddles
With no depth
No longer a deep end
In the pools of our lives
Discipline
Attention
Appreciation

Gratitude

Humanity

All single servings

Like our morning cup of coffee

Disposable.

LA WALKER

Moment of Silence

Can we please have a moment of silence,
For all the broken hearts around the world.
And can we please have a moment to mourn,
For the hearts that are with us no more.
You see I relate to those of the fallen.
Cause they were bold enough
To take that leap of faith
Loving genuine and hard
Keeping the faith until the bitter end
When the reaper comes for their soul.
For a soul without the will to love
Is not a soul considered alive.
They'll lose the ability to be happy,
Life begins to dull and fade,
And though you try save them.
Pounding on their chest trying desperately
To resuscitate the lifeless soul
But in some cases it's far too late.
If we as people in the world,
Continue to hurt without
Picking up the pieces of the broken hearts,
Soon there will be none left
And not a soul in sight.

Margie Wildblood

Ashes

I rest in the foyer, where I watch you greet visitors,
observe the weather when you open the front door.
From the TV close by I listen to you listen to music,
nightly news, Jeopardy, or a movie.

I watch you come and go to the mailbox,
leave and return from your neighborhood walk,
wave goodbye and throw kisses to
departing family and friends.

I am with you in the house
as you go about your day.
My spirit feels your mood, not just
the sorrow of my absence, but also
your laughter as you phone friends,
encourage those who grieve a loss,
as you grieve mine.

I see you glance at shadows,
thinking they are the cat's tail
ducking down the hall,
or is it me you think you see?

At night, I watch you climb the stairs to bed,
long for your warm embrace,
recall your breath on my face as you
whisper softly that you love me.

Thank you for keeping me with you
– the place I always want to be.

Robyn Witt

Mrs. Harris's Secret

Mrs. Harris keeps a secret
behind her garden wall.
She tends it with the pride
of a priestess preparing her altar,
the defiance of a dissident
distributing samizdat,
the pugnacity of a punk lifting
her longest fingers
to the police.
It's not a marijuana plant,
nor a diorama of human bones
on display in her she-shed,
not even dirty films on VHS
hidden in a cavity
beneath her paving stones.
She keeps it in the corner
of the fence,
where not even the longest necks can crane
to catch her cleaning
and restocking her contraband.
Even if her neighbors betray her
to the HOA, she won't give up
her Unapproved Exterior Ornament

(a wire bird feeder).
She won't forsake the birds
fluttering down like flecks
of paint from every dawn,
bearing songs of thanks
in their beaks.

ANDREA YARBOUGH

Priorities

the thing that i need
we all quickly agreed
is more shelf space to store
all the Books i adore.
each one beautifully bound;
no storing these on the ground!
so i hope you don't mind
if i ignore you to find
a new crevice or nook
just the size of a Book.

About the Authors

After a career as a federal manager in Washington DC, **Joanne Alfano** retired to Lakeland, Florida with her life partner. Her work has appeared in several anthologies including previous editions of *NOVA Bards*. She enjoys family, writing and reading, old movies, and creative play with her granddaughter.

Michelle Baker

My career continues to be all about telling people's stories. As a journalist, I tried to tell the truth and nothing but the truth. Now, I decided to turn the stories into short emotional poems to describe relationships. The reader can put themselves in the the poems. Or they can decide if the "speaker" is discussing a lost love or a former family member lost to death.

Dennis Barnes lives in the Northern Virginia area where he leads a not-so-quiet poetic life. He was the 2005 recipient of the Baltimore People's Poetry Done the Most to Advance Poetry award. Mr. Barnes has had poems published in over forty magazines and anthologies. *Shades of Light*, his first book of poetry, was published in 2007.

Raised on a rice and catfish farm in eastern Arkansas, **CL Bledsoe** is the author of more than twenty-five books, including the poetry collections *Riceland, The Bottle Episode*, and his newest, *Driving Around, Looking in Other People's Windows*, as well as his latest novels

Goodbye, Mr. Lonely and *The Saviors*. Bledsoe lives in northern Virginia with his daughter.

KC Bosch is a writer, photographer, and carpenter. A graduate of TJ before it became a fancy science school. He lives about an hour west of DC these days. Making new things and fixing old ones.

An enthusiast of simply delicious moments**, Sheelagh Cabalda** is a heartful activist and mindful writer. Inspired by the Filipino value of kapwa, sacred interconnectedness, she writes to focus on her emotional truth. Born and raised in Jersey City (NJ), she has lived in northern Virginia for seven years with her family and rescue dog, Creagh.

Adina Cassal grew up in several countries and is bilingual (Spanish/English). She works providing human services to people she deeply respects. She enjoys writing about her observations and reflections. Her poetry has appeared in online journals and in anthologies.

Hi, my name is **Luciano Castellani**, a 23 year old Spanish American poet living in Woodbridge Virginia. I began writing poetry after my first heart-break in high school. At the rate I'm going, I'll have a finished book by next year (queue laughter). During my college years, I participated in the Northern Virginia Community College Coffee Shop Poetry Slam where I won an award for having written and performed the best piece at the event.

Mike Croghan works with code by day, which has more in common with poetry than you might think. Mike's first poetry chapbook, *Body* *and Soul*, was published by Local Gems Press in 2018. You can read more of his work at freesourfruit.com.

Anant Dhavale writes poetry as it occurs to him in many languages and forms. His poems have appeared in American anthologies and journals such as the Bourgeon magazine, Poets to Come, Novabards, Spilled Ink, and Poets Anonymous to mention a few. Many of his Marathi and Urdu language poems have appeared in literary journals from India. Anant lives in Herndon, VA with his wife and son.

Rudy Diaz, 20 years old in the Dale city area

A.M. Donovan Currently lives in Virginia, has lived in many places. Everyone has to have a hobby or six. :-)

Danielle Erwin is a Catholic wife and mother who homeschools and enjoys writing poetry whenever the Holy Spirit inspires her. She has published two books of poetry that can be found on Amazon: Holding On: Poetry on Coping With *Loss After Miscarriage* and *Something More: Poetic Moments With God. She* has also published some of her poetry through the Blessed Is She blog.

Robert Fleming lives in Lewes, DE. Published in United States, Canada, England, Ireland and Australia. Member of the Rehoboth Beach, Eastern Shore, and Horror Writer's Association. 2022 winner of San Gabriel Valley CA broadside-1 poem, 2021 winner of Best of Mad Swirl poetry and twice nominated for Pushcart Prize and Best of the Net. Follow Robert at https://www.facebook.com/robert.fleming.5030 .

Rich Follett is a middle school Theatre Arts teacher who has been writing poems and songs for more than fifty years. His poems have been featured in numerous online and print journals. He is the Poet Laureate for Strasburg, VA. Three volumes of poetry are available through NeoPoiesis Press (www.neopoiesispress.com).

Eric Forsbergh's poetry has appeared in *JAMA*, *The Northern Virginia Review, Streetlight, Artemis*, and multiple other venues, including the Arlington County Bus System. He is a retired health care worker and was a volunteer vaccinator against COVID for Loudoun County.

Kimberly Gilliam was born in Northern Virginia and has lived most of her life in the community of Warrenton, Virginia. In addition to writing Poetry, she is a Singer-Songwriter. She has held positions in local churches using her skills to lead Contemporary Worship. Kimberly holds a degree from University of Mary Washington in Music. Her interests in healing and alternative medicine led her to recently become a Licenced Massage Therapist. She specializes in Therapeutic and Cranio-Sacral Massage, Reiki and Sound Healing and now lives in Asheville, North Carolina.

Leigh Giza enjoys writing, especially poetry. She has published three poetry-based books: *Found and Lost, Then and Now, and The Forlorn Heart*. Her blog can be found at https://poemsmostly.wordpress.com/

Katherine Gotthardt, M.Ed. has been writing, editing and teaching for more than 20 years. With ten books to her name, one an Amazon best-selling new release and another a Nonfiction Writers Association Silver Award winner, she pens poetry, children's books and prose from her home in Northern Virginia. She uses proceeds from book sales to benefit community give-back initiatives and can often be found volunteering and supporting other writers in her spare time. Learn more at www.katherinegotthardt.com.

Cathy Hailey teaches in Johns Hopkins University's MA in Teaching Writing program and previously taught high school English and Creative Writing. She is Northern Region Vice President of The Poetry Society of Virginia and organizes In the Company of Laureates. Her chapbook, *I'd Rather Be a Hyacinth*, is forthcoming in 2023.

Nick Hale is the founder and leader of NoVA Bards and the Northern Virginia Poetry Group. He is a member of the Poetry Society of Virginia and a co-founder and the current vice president of the Bards Initiative, a Long Island based poetry nonprofit. Formerly both a literal and metaphorical hat collector, these days, Nick only collects metaphorical hats. He is a partner, publisher, editor, and author with Local Gems Press and has worked on several anthologies including the best-selling *Sound of Solace*. In addition to writing, editing, and performing poetry, Nick enjoys teaching poetry and has given several seminars, panels, and workshops on various poetic topics. In his own poetry, he often enjoys humor and experimenting with different styles, which may make him seem, at times, like he has yet to find his voice. A former almost-teacher, Nick earned a BA in English and an M.Ed in Secondary Education before deciding he didn't want to teach, teaching himself the basics of IT and web design, and then doing neither of those things. Along with James P. Wagner, Nick co-authored *Japanese Poetry Forms: A Poet's Guide*. He is the author of *Broken Reflections* and three upcoming chapbooks which, he claims haven't been published yet only because he's too busy working on books that are not his.

Deborah Hartman enjoys writing, felting and propagating houseplants in Arlington, Virginia. She has learned that the adage "Once You Learn to Ride a Bicycle You Never Forget" does not apply in her case.

Danni Hill A young undergraduate woman in her twenties who loves to write and read with a Starbucks drink as her muse.

Tim Hoffman is a Northern Virginia resident since 2004. He has been an educator throughout his adult life. He had been a member of Nagoya Writes, an English-language writers group in central Japan.

Emilio Iasiello has published four novels, a collection of short stories, and a full-length book of poetry. He has published poetry in several university and literary journals and written the screenplays for several independent feature films and short films and has had stage plays produced in the United States and United Kingdom.

Jodie James is a 22-year-old poet living in Northern Virginia. Her poems have been published in Indiana University's 2020 *CANVAS Creative Arts Magazine* and *NoVA Bards 2021: An Anthology of Northern Virginia Poetry*.

Richard Eric Johnson lives and writes poetry in Arlington, Virginia. He has authored four full-length poetry collections and his poetry has appeared in numerous online and print journals. Eric is also a Pushcart nominee. He is a graduate of Indiana University with a B.A. in

Germanic Languages and an M.S. in Education. After a tour in Viet Nam and West Berlin, he embarked on a career as a public servant and is now very happily retired.

Kathy Walden Kaplan, a sculptor, printmaker, author and naturalist, has lived in Reston since 1983. She is the author *of THE DOG OF KNOTS, a children's middle grade novel* about *the Yom Kippur War*. She studied at the Albert Schweitzer College in Switzerland and received her degree in Studio Art from the University of California at Santa Barbara. Her handmade and artist books are in many collections including the Beinecke Rare Book and Manuscript Library at Yale University, the Stanford University Library and Special Collections at UCSB Library.

Leah Kim is a current resident of Northern Virginia. Her writing is diverse, including many styles of poetry and prose. Besides writing, she enjoys listening to Taylor Swift, spending times with loved ones, and enjoying the Virginia nature. She can be found on Instagram @lskim-writing

Kathleen Kinsolving composed and performed rap songs in the 1980s. 25 years later she wrote and published two non-fiction books. She's also written screenplays, film essays, and a play. Kathleen has taught poetry to secondary students since 2008, and started writing her own poems in 2019.

Lucy Koons is a Virginia native who has lived more than 20 years abroad, mostly in Lebanon and Qatar. Koons is a writer and editor who began her career in Washington, DC, on Capitol Hill. Overseas she worked at The American University of Beirut and Georgetown University in Qatar. Koons's favorite activity is going on adventures with her husband and daughter.

Tori Kovarik is a poet and visual artist living in northern Virginia. From 2013-2016 she served as the Poet Laureate of the city of Alexandria. As well as having done numerous poetry readings and performances, Tori has published two collections of poetry

Tisha Kramer is an artist, poet, and mother. She has been a resident in NoVA for 5 years and enjoys the rich history of the area. She enjoys sharing her life's passion through various methods of expression such as dance, writing, poetry, and music.

Karen Krotzer wrote her first poems in the 4th grade and kept writing after that. She has even written poems for her elementary school students to assist them in learning sight words and other literacy components as well as for family and friends over the years. She was an active staff member of and a contributor to both her high school and her college literary and art magazines. She is grateful to her high school creative writing teacher for recommending her for a scholarship to the Lebanon Valley College Youth Scholars creative writing summer institute between her junior and senior years. She has had work previously published in her school magazines and with her fellow scholars at Lebanon Valley College as well as by Great Lakes Poetry Press, the Tom Byrd Institute, Hutton Publications, and Local Gems Press.

Marcia Leftwich is an inspirational writer and motivational speaker who focuses on finding the silver lining versus feeling the weight of the rain from a storm cloud. Her writing and podcast provide encouragement to learn from the valleys in life and to climb the mountain and stake the victory flag. One of her guiding principles is to allow her life and story to empower others to not just survive but thrive. When she is not writing, she is involved in counseling, mentoring and teaching yoga and meditation.

K. A. Lewis graduated from the Corcoran School of Art in 1986. Her work experience includes cake decorating, jewelry sales, a hypnosis certification, being robbed at gunpoint, and 32 years as a custom picture framer. She writes poetry, fantasy, and SF, and since 2014, her work has been published in twenty anthologies. Katy and her husband live with four demanding cats in a small book-stuffed house in Falls Church, VA.

Pardee Lowe, Jr. is a poet from Falls Church, VA. He has a BA, MA, and PhD in German all from UC, Berkeley. His themes are Nature, Humankind, Aging, and the Spirit. He has published two books of Quaker poetry, and single poems in *NoVa Bards, One Art, Spillwords, The Front Porch*, and *Trouvaille Review*.

Louis Mateus started to share his poetry publicly after many years of cultivating the craft of poetry privately while launching his career in the mental health field. He has been published in various publications: *The Federal Poet, The Listening Eye, Skidrow Penthouse, The Writer's Guide*, Published by the Writers Center in Bethesda, Maryland, and previous Anthologies of Northern Virginia Bards among them. He is an avid reader of poetry, believing this to be the key to good writing, and is very much interested in the therapeutic properties of poetry, in study and practice.

Sindhu Mathew lives in Northern Virginia with her family and works as a Marketing Specialist at George Mason University. Her poems have been previously published by Local Gems Press and some have found their way into music.

Megan McDonald started writing in a junior high school creative writing class in Hawaii, but other than yearly Christmas poems did not start writing for twenty years. She credits her restart to poetry to an article in the Washington Post about a long running Virginia poetry venue. After attending a meeting of Poets Anonymous in 1995 she generated two poems and has been writing ever since. She has been published in *Poets Anonymous* (Virginia) anthologies, *Poet's Anonymous (*United Kingdom) anthology, *Poetry Just for you, Event Horizon*, *Poets Domain* and *NovaBard*s. She currently is a co-host of Poets Anonymous, a long running Northern Virginia open reading.

Alan Meyrowitz has published in *The Literary Hatchet, Lucid Rhythms, The Nassau Review, Poetry Quarterly*, and others. In 2013 and 2015 the Science Fiction Poetry Association nominated his poems for a Dwarf Star Award.

Liz Milner is a native Washingtonian who has written for a wide range of local governments and non-profits. She presently works for the Arlington County Public Library. She earned a Master of Arts Degree in Political Theory from the University of Chicago, so she has firm grasp of "alternative facts." She is currently working on an English translation of Akira Kurosawa's Ran, tentative title is *Also Ran*. She lives in Annandale, VA.

Adrienne Nguyen is a Northern Virginia native currently living in Prince William County. Her literary heroes are Walt Whitman, William Carlos Williams, T.S. Eliot, and Neil Gaiman. She writes for the pleasure of seeing words on paper and to, sometimes, unburden her heart.

Susan Rexroad began writing poetry in her car at red lights, answering the call to stop and write what needed to be written. She has expanded her writing venues to lounge chairs, tubs, countertops and more! She enjoys participating in several poetry groups through George Mason University's Osher Lifetime Learning Institute where she facilitates a poetry reading club.

Govinda Giri Prerana, born in 1958 at Tekkar Bhansari, Makwanpur, Nepal is a renowned poet, lyricist, novelist and storywriter. He made his debut in writing in 1977 with the publication of his story "Kinara". He now has six story collections to his credit and six novels. His collections of poems include *Phoolharu Kehi ta Bola, Swapnakatha Jaari Chha, Achanak Ekcdin, Rajmargaka Sundariharoo,* and *Dui Dashakka Aawajharoo*. He has also published three collections of travel essays, two collection of essays. He has also contributed a number of stories to various collections, periodicals and journals. His poems has been translated in Hindi, Bengali, Malay and Turkish. He lives in Falls Church, Virginia.

Susan Rexroad began writing poetry in her car at red lights, answering the call to stop and write what needed to be written. She has expanded her writing venues to lounge chairs, tubs, countertops and more! She enjoys participating in several poetry groups through George Mason University's Osher Lifetime Learning Institute where she facilitates a poetry reading club.

Jim Sanders Since retiring from the federal government in 2012, I have devoted my time to trumpet-playing, poetry, and planting native species.

Aparna Sanjay is a relatively recent import to Northern Virginia and has lived in various parts of India and USA. Her poetry draws upon these varied cultural influences and also her work in the nonprofit sector, where she helps social impact organizations grow and scale. She has been published in various online journals.

Judith Shapiro is a Northern Virginia writer who spends part of the year on the opposite coast, marveling at the sun that sets instead of rising. When the novel she's writing looks the other way, she secretly writes anything else. Her work has appeared in *Pigeon Review, Moss Piglet, Microfiction Monday Magazine, The Sun* and many others.

Ron Shapiro holds a BA from the University of Delaware and an M.A. in the Teaching of Writing from Northeastern University. An award-winning retired FCPS English and Creative Writing teacher with over 40 years of classroom experience, he now teaches Memoir Writing at OLLI through George Mason University. In 2011, he received Cornell University's Outstanding Teacher Award. He has published articles in The Whole Word Catalogue and More Strategies for Teaching Writing.

Leslie Sinclair is a well-educated woman who had the temerity to believe her expensive education would be so valuable to the working world that special accommodations would be made for her most unfortunate disability – i.e., the presence in her life of a husband and children. What a princess, the world seemed to say. Perhaps she should have abandoned her family and applied herself, instead, to the pursuit of economic growth.

K.S. Taylor-Barnes is a native Virginian, former military spouse, and retired Fairfax County high school English teacher. She is a member of Local Gems and was published in the *NoVA Bards 2021* anthology. She is currently working on her first book-length manuscript of poetry.

Sally Toner is a High School English teacher who has lived in the Washington, D.C. area for over 25 years. Her poetry, fiction, and non-fiction have appeared in *Northern Virginia Magazine, Gargoyle Magazine, District Lit, Watershed Review, Porcupine Lit,* and other publications. She lives in Reston, Virginia with her husband and two daughters. Her first chapbook, *Anansi and Friends*, from Finishing Line Press, is a mixed genre work focusing on diagnosis, treatment, and recovery from breast cancer. She can be found at SallyToner.com and on Twitter @SallyToner.

Lesley Tyson is from Reston, Virginia, has had work in issues *of The Poet's Domain, NoVA Bards Anthology and Poets Anonymous-25* and *Beyond Anthology, CHAOS A Poetry Vortex, Spilled Ink: A Poetry Anthology, and Fairfax County Poetry Review: Virginia Bards*. Lesley is also co-editor of *The Hands We Hold; Poetry Concerning Breast Cancer* along with Long Island poet, Kate Fox. Lesley's first book of poetry:

journey through red heaven was released in 2019. She also has two mini-chapbooks: what never changes and a stone in the rain-49 haiku. Lesley is a regular contributor to several local Northern Virginia poetry groups and co-leads Poets Anonymous ©, Northern Virginia's longest running open reading.

Rebecca Visger is an artist and sometimes poet born and raised in Northern Virginia. Her work tends to be dramatic, enigmatic, and at least a bit fantastical. Her poems and paintings tiptoe the line between real and surreal.

James P. Wagner (Ishwa) is an editor, publisher, award-winning fiction writer, essayist, historian performance poet, and alum twice over (BA & MALS) of Dowling College. He is the publisher for Local Gems Poetry Press and the Senior Founder and President of the Bards Initiative. He is also the founder and Grand Laureate of Bards Against Hunger, a series of poetry readings and anthologies dedicated to gathering food for local pantries that operates in over a dozen states. His most recent individual collection of poetry is *Everyday Alchemy*. He was the Long Island, NY National Beat Poet Laureate from 2017-2019. He was the Walt Whitman Bicentennial Convention Chairman and teaches poetry workshops at the Walt Whitman Birthplace State Historic Site. James has edited over 60 poetry anthologies and hosted book launch events up and down the East Coast. He was named the National Beat Poet Laureate of the United States from 2020-2021. He is the owner-operator of the Dog-Eared Bard's Book Shop In New York.

Margie Wildblood grew up in Salem, Virginia. She earned degrees in English, Psychology, and Counseling. She retired from Northern Virginia Community College in 2019. She resides in Fairfax County.

Robyn Witt grew up in North Carolina and currently lives in Herndon, Virginia. Her poems have been published in the literary magazines *Copy Write* (R. J. Reynolds High School) and *The Gleaner* (Delaware Valley University). When she is not writing poetry, you might find her riding her bike, geocaching, or watching the geese at Fairfax Lake.

Andrea Yarbough is a high school English Language Arts teacher in Nokesville, VA. A lifelong book-lover, it is only recently that Andrea has begun to identify as a writer as well. This represents her first meaningful foray into the world of poetry.

NoVA Bards 2023

Opens for Submissions
March 1st 2023!
Submit up to 3 poems of 100 or fewer lines each (or one long poem)
to
novabards@gmail.com

Include your submission both as a single attachment and in the body
of the e-mail.

Include a 3-4 line 3rd person bio with your poems.
Submissions open to both all current and former residents of
Northern Virginia and to non-residents who are members of the
Northern Virginia Poetry Group and have attended at least one NoVA
Bards event.

Local Gems Poetry Press is a small Long Island, NY based poetry press dedicated to spreading poetry through performance and the written word. Local Gems believes in building local poetry communities through publications and events.

Local Gems has published over 300 titles.

www.localgemspoetrypress.com

Made in the USA
Middletown, DE
30 October 2022

13800445R00076